Pin and Tuck It!

Written by Jillian Powell
Photographed by Tim Platt

Collins

It is on a rack.

2

I pick it.

It is red.

4

I pin it up.

It is a top.

6

I tuck it in.

It is a cap.

8

I tip it.

It is a sock.

I tug it up.

It is tin.

12

I tap it.

I put it on

pin

tuck

tip

tap

tug

15

Ideas for reading

Written by Clare Dowdall, PhD
Lecturer and Primary Literacy Consultant

Learning objectives: *(reading objectives correspond with Pink B band; all other objectives correspond with Purple band)* read simple words by sounding out and blending the phonemes all through the word from left to right; recognise common digraphs; draw together ideas and information from across a whole text; use syntax and context to build their store of vocabulary when reading for meaning; explain ideas and processes using imaginative and adventurous vocabulary and non-verbal gestures to support communication

Curriculum links: History

Focus phonemes: s, a, t, p, i, n, m, d, g, o, ck, e, u, r

Resources: whiteboard, magnetic letters, paper, pens

Word count: 44

Getting started

- Look at the picture on the front cover and read the title. Ask children to talk about dressing-up activities that they have played and what they like to dress up as.

- Ask children to write the words *pin* and *tuck* on a whiteboard and add sound buttons. Notice that for the digraph *ck* there is just one sound, but two letters.

- Turn to the blurb. Ask children to read the text aloud. Support children to blend the sounds in the word *p-i-ck*. Discuss what *I pick it* means.

Reading and responding

- Turn to pp2–3. Ask children to read the text. Challenge children to blend the phonemes *r-a-ck* to read the new word. Model rereading the sentences on pp2–3 fluently.

- Ask children to read to p13 independently, pausing at each page to notice what the children are wearing. Encourage them to blend phonemes to read new words.

- Listen as children read. Praise them for blending through words and rereading for fluency.